# Praise for *Get to the Point!*

MW01038602

"Schwartzberg sketches out a simple tool kit on how to know, make, and sell your point. His book is worth a close read."
   —**Hari Sreenivasan, Anchor and Senior Correspondent,** *PBS NewsHour*

"Joel Schwartzberg's step-by-step guide will help you find your point, hone it, and deliver it powerfully."
   —**Mark Ragan, CEO, Ragan Communications**

"If every speaker absorbed the contents of this wee volume, every speech would be a vital speech."
   —**David Murray, Editor and Publisher,** *Vital Speeches of the Day*, **and Executive Director, Professional Speechwriters Association**

"*Get to the Point!* delivers on its promise, enabling you to effectively get to, stick to, and make your point. The lessons enabled me to communicate more effectively to my employees, clients, and vendors."
   —**Jeremy Miller, founder and CEO, FSAstore.com/HSAstore.com**

"This should be required reading whether you're presenting an annual report, a book report, or anything in between. It's that simple, incisive, and applicable!"
   —**Douglass Hatcher, Vice President, Executive Communications, Mastercard**

"This quick guide will help any busy professional become a more persuasive and effective speaker."
   —**Lowell Weiss, former presidential speechwriter for Bill Clinton**

"Chock full of clearly written, easy-to-apply tips, *Get to the Point!* is a no-nonsense guide to communicating efficiently and effectively."
   —**Monique Visintainer, Senior Director, Executive Communications, and Speechwriter for the President, Concur**

"Finally, a book with actionable tools that show you how to make a point and stick to it. If you have something important to say, take Joel's advice and use it."
   —**Allison Shapira, founder and CEO, Global Public Speaking LLC, and Harvard Kennedy School lecturer**

"Business leaders everywhere should buy copies of this book and dole them out like candy to their teams to see their communication capabilities transform overnight."
—**Allison Hemming, founder and CEO, The Hired Guns**

"I would recommend this book to anyone who wants to be a better, more effective communicator."
—**Risa Weinstock, President and CEO, Animal Care Centers of NYC**

"*Get to the Point!* presents simple solutions to help salespeople sell, managers manage, leaders lead, and influencers influence."
—**Josh Steimle, founder and CEO, MWI, and author of *Chief Marketing Officers at Work***

"If I were forced to select only one book for all the technical presenters I've coached through the years, this would be it."
—**Dianna Booher, bestselling author of *Communicate Like a Leader* and *Creating Personal Presence***

"*Get to the Point!* practices what it teaches. It's a joy to read, and it's also funny. What's not to like?"
—**Sam Horn, CEO, The Intrigue Agency, and author of *Got Your Attention?***

"Joel provided one of the most user-friendly trainings I have received in my professional career. I would highly recommend him and his book for experienced and novice communicators and pretty much anyone in between."
—**Daniel Elbaum, Assistant Executive Director, American Jewish Committee**

"*Get to the Point!* offers a blueprint for the formulation and delivery of effective points, and the incorporation of humor makes this guide a quick and pleasant read."
—**Will Baker, Director, Global Debate Initiative, New York University, and Chief Information Officer, Baker Consulting Associates**

"The strategies will force you to rethink every presentation and help you make your point more effectively. I loved it."
—**Fauzia Burke, President, FSB Associates, and author of *Online Marketing for Busy Authors***

# Get to the Point!

# Get to the Point!

## *Sharpen* Your Message and Make Your Words *Matter*

### JOEL SCHWARTZBERG

**BK**

Berrett–Koehler Publishers, Inc.
*a BK Business book*

Copyright © 2017 Joel Schwartzberg

All rights reserved. No part of this publication may be reproduced, distributed, or transmitted in any form or by any means, including photocopying, recording, or other electronic or mechanical methods, without the prior written permission of the publisher, except in the case of brief quotations embodied in critical reviews and certain other noncommercial uses permitted by copyright law. For permission requests, write to the publisher, addressed "Attention: Permissions Coordinator," at the address below.

Berrett-Koehler Publishers, Inc.
1333 Broadway, Suite 1000,
Oakland, CA 94612-1921
Tel: (510) 817-2277   Fax: (510) 817-2278   www.bkconnection.com

ORDERING INFORMATION

Quantity sales. Special discounts are available on quantity purchases by corporations, associations, and others. For details, contact the "Special Sales Department" at the Berrett-Koehler address above.

Individual sales. Berrett-Koehler publications are available through most bookstores. They can also be ordered directly from Berrett-Koehler: Tel: (800) 929-2929; Fax: (802) 864-7626; www.bkconnection.com

Orders for college textbook/course adoption use. Please contact Berrett-Koehler: Tel: (800) 929-2929; Fax: (802) 864-7626.

Orders by U.S. trade bookstores and wholesalers. Please contact Ingram Publisher Services, Tel: (800) 509-4887; Fax: (800) 838-1149; E-mail: customer service@ingrampublisherservices.com; or visit www.ingrampublisherservices .com/Ordering for details about electronic ordering.

Berrett-Koehler and the BK logo are registered trademarks of Berrett-Koehler Publishers, Inc.

Printed in the United States of America

Berrett-Koehler books are printed on long-lasting acid-free paper. When it is available, we choose paper that has been manufactured by environmentally responsible processes. These may include using trees grown in sustainable forests, incorporating recycled paper, minimizing chlorine in bleaching, or recycling the energy produced at the paper mill.

Cataloging-in-Publication Data is available at the Library of Congress

ISBN: 978-1-52309-411-0

FIRST EDITION

22 21 20 19 18 17    10 9 8 7 6 5 4 3 2 1

Cover design: Maureen Forys, Happenstance Type-O-Rama
Cover photo: Shaun Wilkinson/Shutterstock
Book design and production: Maureen Forys, Happenstance Type-O-Rama
Copyediting: Rebecca Rider, Happenstance Type-O-Rama
Proofreader: Elizabeth Welch, Happenstance Type-O-Rama

*Dedicated to the hundreds of students and clients who came to me with soft ideas and left with sharp points.*

# Acknowledgments

Thanks to the key Schwartzbergs in my life—my wife Anne; my kids Evan, Mylie, and Josie; and my parents Howard and Susan—for their unconditional love and support.

Also thanks to the crack team at Berrett-Koehler, especially Neal Maillet and Jeevan Sivasubramaniam for their encouragement and expert guidance.

# Contents

If you can't explain it simply, you don't understand it well enough.

—Albert Einstein

# Introduction

**W**hen I was in sixth grade, I gave one of my first formal speeches. Wearing a blue three-piece suit and wide clip-on tie, I competed at a forensics tournament and gave a speech about the neutron bomb, a now-obsolete device designed to minimize property destruction while maximizing human destruction through radiation.

I know, fun stuff for an 11-year-old.

When asked what my speech was about, I simply said, "The neutron bomb." It was a classic book report: lots of information about what I cheekily called an "explosive" issue, yet it took no position on the issue whatsoever.

I think about that speech often—not just because it was the beginning of a thrilling competitive journey I would continue for the next 11 years—but because it also represents the biggest mistake people make in public communication: sharing information, but not selling a point.

I see that little me in many of my students and clients: important and talented people with critical things to say, yet who deliver simple "who, what, where" book reports, or simply ramble with no clear direction.

These are salespeople who never say, "This product will increase your profits," activists who never say, "This approach will save lives," designers who never say, "This style will inspire interest," and business leaders who never say, "This system will make us more efficient."

One could wave an accusing finger at our educational system, our media models, even our parenting styles, but I'm less interested in *why* people are making too many speeches and too few points; I'm more interested in helping them identify and successfully convey their points.

I ended my competitive public speaking career with a national championship in 1990, and what I learned during that time and even more since then is this: no matter who you are, how you're communicating, or who you're communicating with, you benefit tremendously from having a point. After all, without one, everything you say is pointless.

No one is better qualified or equipped to make your specific points than you are, so I hope this book elevates your ability to effectively champion your ideas.

# 1

# The Big Flaw

In more than ten years as a strategic communications trainer, I've seen one fatal presentation flaw more often than any other. It's a flaw that contributes directly to nervousness, rambling, and, ultimately, epic failure, and most speakers have no idea that this flaw is ruining their presentations:

They don't have a point.

They have what they think is a point, but it's actually something much less.

And here's the deal:

- ► You have to have a point to make a point.

- ► You have to have a point to sell your point.

- ► You have to have a point to stay on point.

Many articles about public presentation shallowly advise you to "have a clear point" or "stick to your topic" but leave it at that. Nowhere have I seen the critical missing piece: how to *formulate* an actual point and *convey it effectively*. It's like a nutritionist simply telling you to "eat well," then handing you a bill. Good luck with that.

The stakes couldn't be higher. Simply put, without a point, you don't know what you're talking about. What you end up with—and what we see so often now in many different settings—is too many people making speeches and not enough people making points.

Once a presenter has a point, the next most important job is to effectively deliver it.

What do I mean by *effectively*? Simple: If the point is received, the presenter succeeds. If the point is not received, the presenter fails—regardless of any other impression made.

As you read this, you're probably imagining a classic public speaker in front of a packed audience. But the truth is, every time you communicate, there's always a potential point. Whether you're giving a conference keynote speech or a Monday morning status report, talking to your mother or your manager, composing an email or creating a Power-Point, having a real point is critical to getting what you most want from that interaction.

This book will help you make the most of those moments by showing you how to identify your point, leverage it, nail it, stick to it, and sell it. It'll also show you how to overcome presentational anxiety and train others to identify and make their own points.

Of course, knowing you need a point is useless if you don't know what a point is . . . and most people don't. Let's start with the basics, kicking off with a famous "I believe."

I believe that unarmed truth and unconditional love will have the final word.

—Martin Luther King, Jr.

# 2

# Know Your Point

**W**e all know a thing or two about points. After all, we refer to points all the time:

"Get to your point!"

"What's your point?"

"Please stick to your point."

Yet all too often, people confuse a point with something else: a theme, a topic, a title, a catchphrase, an idea. We believe a good speech can simply be about supply-side economics, the benefits of athleticism, the role of stepmothers, or the summer you spent in Costa Rica.

But none of these are actual points.

Imagine a child's history paper on the American Revolution. If you asked him for his point, he might say it's about the American Revolution.

That's a topic.

He might also say it's about George Washington and the Founding of America.

That's a title.

He might even say it's about the role of perseverance in American history.

That's a theme.

But a point is unique.

A point is a contention you can propose, argue, defend, illustrate, and prove.

A point makes clear its value and its purpose.

And to maximize impact, a point should be sold, not just shared or described.

So what does a true point look like? It should look something like this:

> **A politician's point:** "My plan will expand home-buying opportunities for the middle class."

> **A CEO's point:** "This investment in R&D will ensure our company continues to stay relevant."

> **A vendor's point:** "My unique services will make you more profitable."

**An advocate's point:** "This movement will save lives."

**A job interviewee's point:** "I will help your department accomplish its goals."

**A mother's point:** "Saving that money now means you'll be able to buy something even bigger later."

A surefire way to know if you have a real point—and successfully create one—is to apply a simple three-step test, followed by two bonus "point-enhancers":

Step One: The "I Believe That" Test

Step Two: The "So What" Test

Step Three: The "Why" Test

Enhancement One: Avoiding Split Ends

Enhancement Two: Adding a Value Proposition

These steps are the bread-and-butter of this book, so you may want to find your highlighter and take breaks to apply these recommendations to your own points and subpoints. The best way to learn these tips is to apply them right away.

## Step One: The "I Believe That" Test

This is a pass/fail test, and it boils down to this:

*Can your point fit into this phrase to form a complete sentence?*

*"I believe that* _____*."*

For example, you can't say, "I believe that the American Revolution." Or "I believe that George Washington and the Founding of America." Or even "I believe that the role of perseverance in American history." These are fragments, not complete sentences, and your fifth-grade English teacher would not be happy.

But you can say, "I believe the American Revolution gave our country an enduring democratic identity."

Some more grown-up examples:

You can't say, "I believe that innovations in IT."

But you can say, "I believe that innovations in IT will make us more efficient."

You can't say, "I believe income inequality."

But you can say, "I believe income inequality is America's biggest domestic challenge."

You can't say, "I believe that investing in infrastructure."

But you can say, "I believe that investing in infrastructure is the best way to prepare for our future."

Try this test right now with a point you occasionally make or might make to your colleagues, boss, or potential clients. Then see if what you thought was your point was really something else.

Once your point passes the "I Believe That" Test, move on to Step Two. If it's not quite there yet, keep working at it until your "I believe that" is grammatically sound. If you need inspiration, read some of the "I Believe" statements that separate the chapters in this book.

## Step Two: The "So What" Test

The "So What" Test roots out points that pass the "I Believe That" test but may be too shallow to serve as the foundation of a meaningful presentation. These weak points are often truisms. A *truism,* by definition, is inarguably true, so there's no use proposing one, whether your point is that "world peace is a good thing" or "ice cream is delicious."

You might also call this the "duh" test.

You can tell if your point is too shallow or a truism by asking two questions: "Is there a reasonable counterpoint?" and "Can I spend more than a minute defending this point?"

More point-focused versions of those earlier examples could be "Ice cream is always a better dessert than frozen yogurt" and "The United Nations is critical to preserving world peace."

These are points that can be argued with support from logic, data, or case studies.

Being able to distinguish between a shallow argument and a substantive one is crucial to making a meaningful point.

Now let's put Steps One and Two together.

### Example One:

"The 2016 Election" = Not a point

*(Flunks the "I Believe That" Test)*

"The 2016 Election was a huge news event." = Not a point

*(Passes the "I Believe That" Test, but it's too shallow—there's no counterpoint.)*

"The 2016 Election changed the conventional rules of running for President." = A point!

*(Passes the "I Believe That" Test and requires analysis to make the case)*

**Example Two:**

"Facebook's new privacy features" = Not a point

*(Flunks the "I Believe That" Test)*

"Facebook has new privacy features." = Not a point

*(Passes the "I Believe That" Test, but it's clearly true.)*

"Facebook's new privacy features substantially protect their users." = A point!

*(Passes the "I Believe That" Test, and it's something worth contending.)*

Almost every professional communication—and even most personal ones—can be improved by highlighting a point. A student once challenged me on this by suggesting that the person who introduces speakers or simply welcomes an audience doesn't have a point.

Indeed, "Introducing Samantha Speaker" isn't a point.

But "Samantha Speaker's ideas will help us become more effective project managers" certainly is.

"Hello and welcome!" isn't a point.

But "The learnings from this conference will make your Human Resources processes more efficient" certainly is.

By this time, you probably have a usable and substantive point—imagine it as the tip of a #2 pencil. But ask yourself this: is it the sharpest point possible? The answer to that will come from Step Three.

## Step Three: The "Why" Test

The "Why" Test is crucial to ensure you're not using meaningless adjectives—what I call "badjectives." These are generic adjectives that only add dead weight to your point.

Compare these two columns of adjectives:

| Column 1 | Column 2 |
|----------|----------|
| Excellent | Urgent |
| Great | Profitable |
| Wonderful | Efficient |
| Amazing | Unprecedented |
| Very Good | Galvanizing |

The adjectives on the left are nearly worthless in comparison to the ones on the right. When we say something is "great" or "very good," there's little indication of scale, reason, or specific meaning. Yet speeches and written reports—and more than a few Tweets—are often loaded with badjectives.

If you're using badjectives, or have a suspicion you are, start the correction by saying your fully realized point aloud.

Next, ask yourself: "Why?" and answer that question.

**Example One:**

I believe hiring a social media manager is important.

*(Why?)*

Because she can help us build positive buzz around our product.

Now eliminate the badjective "important," and connect the first part ("I believe hiring a social media manager . . . ") directly to the last part (" . . . can help us build positive buzz around our product."):

I believe a social media manager can build critical buzz around our product.

**Example Two:**

I believe our marketing strategy is weak.

*(Why?)*

Because it focuses too much on product benefits and not enough on customer needs.

Like in the previous example, connect the first part directly to the last part, eliminating the badjective "weak":

I believe our marketing strategy focuses too much on product benefits and not enough on customer needs.

Audit your presentation materials constantly to root out badjectives and replace them with more meaningful adjectives.

Better yet, don't use an adjective at all and make the point through example.

For example:

**Not Good:**

"Adopting this protocol will be great for our company."

**Good:**

"Adopting this protocol will be very productive for our company."

**Better:**

"Adopting this protocol will allow our operations to run more efficiently."

All points, but which makes the strongest case to you?

Using badjectives is like when a Little League coach says "Come on now, Johnnie!" versus "Keep your eye on the ball as it comes to you, Johnnie!" One has little-to-no value, whereas the other makes a useful point.

Remember: You don't want to be your point's cheerleader; you want to be its champion.

## Enhancement One: Avoiding Split Ends

Often, a speaker will sneak two or more points into one using "split ends":

*I believe moving our files to the cloud will (1) improve our carbon footprint and (2) make us more efficient.*

If your point suffers from split ends, no shampoo will help. Whatever you gain by squeezing in multiple ideas, you lose twice over by diluting the impact of each. The audience is not only forced to divide its attention among multiple points but is also given no direction as to which idea is most relevant.

In most cases, you can spot the strongest one based on your organization's mission and your audience's highest interests.

In this case, "make us more efficient" is likely stronger than "improve our carbon footprint" because "efficient" speaks to cost savings, higher productivity, and higher profits, whereas "carbon footprint" connects mostly to specific environmental concerns. (Of course, if you're at an environmental conference, flip that priority.)

Whatever specific idea you choose, know that removing a detail from your point doesn't mean it must be banished from your presentation. There's always room in a presentation to include multiple elements as "added benefits" or "extra considerations," but the key is to avoid details and words that detract from your main point.

## Enhancement Two: Adding a Value Proposition

In many cases, you can enhance your point by incorporating the *highest value proposition*. What's the greatest impact your idea will effect? It may be a way to cut costs, a way to help low-income children succeed in school, a way to sell more toasters, or a way to save lives, but your audience—not just you—must recognize it as a substantive benefit.

Compare these points, which pass Steps One and Two:

> (I believe) this measure will enable us to make smarter financial decisions.

> (I believe) my educational proposal will raise student test scores.

> (I believe) this approach will improve our marketing effectiveness.

> (I believe) this innovation will optimize hospital operations.

to these:

> (I believe) this measure will dramatically cut our costs.

> (I believe) my proposal will help low-income children succeed in school.

> (I believe) this approach will enable us to sell more toasters.

> (I believe) this innovation will save more lives.

In too many communications, declarations don't go as far as they can to achieve full impact. If your idea can save lives, protect the peace, or make tons of money, why not use those magic words to sell your point? Push yourself beyond positive metrics and short-term benefits to sell the ultimate goal—the stuff of your hopes and dreams, not of your To Do lists and status reports. This will truly activate your audience.

## Don't Get Attached to the Words

Last tip: Don't get too attached to the words. Some point-makers—especially writers and lawyers—write a "perfect point" and then treat it like gospel or a set-in-concrete mission statement. This tactic comes with some peril: if you forget some of those precise words midway through your point, your presentation may go off the rails because you didn't give yourself room to improvise. Your true goal as a communicator is to convey your point, not a precise arrangement of words, so feel free to use your vocabulary flexibly—just be sure your point remains concise.

Now let's put all of these ideas together in two real-world examples:

### Example I: NPR Pledge Drive

If you listen to NPR regularly, you may dread the pledge drives—extended periods when they often steal airtime to ask for donations. It's annoying and repetitive, but necessary to meet their financial goals. Below is an evolution of that donation point from a relatively flat point to its most powerful incarnation, and the prompts that take it there.

You should donate to public radio.

*(Why should I?)*

Donating to public radio is important.

*(Why is it important?)*

Donating to public radio supports quality programming.

*(Which does what?)*

Donating to public radio helps expose vital truths.

*(Where do I send the check?)*

There's a dramatic difference in impact between "You should donate to public radio" and "Donating to public radio helps expose vital truths." The point immediately elevates from a generic plea to an urgent proposal. That's the power of the point.

## Example 2: Taylor vs. Denzel

If you want to see clear consequences of knowing and not knowing your points, check out these award acceptance speeches from two of our biggest entertainment superstars. (They're easy to find and watch on YouTube).

Start with the end of Taylor Swift's February 15, 2016 speech accepting the Grammy Award for Album of the Year. It went like this:

> *As the first woman to win Album of the Year at the Grammys twice, I want to say to all the young women out there: There are going to be people along the way who will try to undercut your success, or take credit for your accomplishments, or your fame. But if you just focus on the work and you don't let those people sidetrack you, someday when you get where you're going, you'll*

*look around and you will know that it was you and the people who love you who put you there, and that will be the greatest feeling in the world. Thank you for this moment.*

Nailed it. A clear and singular "I believe that." A clear value presentation. No rambling—she got in and out efficiently. I'm not sure if Taylor memorized that speech or not, but she clearly knew the point she wanted to make, and made it effectively.

Now compare that speech to one by Denzel Washington accepting the prestigious Cecil B. DeMille Award at the 2016 Golden Globe Awards in January 2016, which went like this:

*Thank you. I lost my speech. Thank you. All right. Sit down. That's good. Thank you. Thank you. I'm missing one. Our Malcolm, filmmaker, he's working on his thesis at AFI. Yeah, he will give you a job one day after me. Yeah, you really do forget everything you're supposed to do. I'm speechless. I just thank you. I thank the Hollywood Foreign Press. Freddie Fields, who first—some of you may know Freddie Fields. He invited me to the first Hollywood Foreign Press luncheon. He said, "They're going to watch the movie. We're going to feed them. They're going to come over. You're going to take pictures with everybody. You're going to hold the magazines, take the pictures, and you're going to win the award." I won that year. I want to thank the Hollywood Foreign Press for supporting me over the years, and they've always made me feel like a friend or part of the party. . . . [After thanking a handful of people] Huh? Yeah, I do need my glasses. You were right. Come here. Who else is on the list? Oh, well, anyway. Man, that's all right. Anyway, God bless you all. I didn't thank the family? Thank the family, and God bless you all. Thank you.*

It's obvious who gave the stronger speech, but what made Taylor's more engaging than Denzel's wasn't a matter of charm, confidence, humor, practice, or even content. It was about having a point, knowing the point, and delivering the point.

No offense to Denzel—one of our greatest living actors and I'm sure a wonderful human being—but if you gave a speech like his in a professional setting, you'd likely never be allowed to speak in public again.

The bottom line is this: The only way to deliver the full value of an idea is by making a true point. And like a quality steak knife, the sharper it is, the more penetrating it will be.

I believe that good journalism, good television, can make our world a better place.

—Christiane Amanpour

# 3

# Make Your Point

Knowing your point is a critical start, but still only part of your overall job. The next part—successfully conveying your point—relies on clearly understanding what your most important job is (and what it's not), and being able to start strong.

## Know Your Job

When we consider the attributes of "great communicators," these qualities—and others like them—traditionally come to mind:

- ► Interesting
- ► Informative

- Funny

- Engaging

- Confident

- Charismatic

- Educational

- Exciting

Some communicators focus heavily on creating these perceptions. Their internal voices say:

"I've got to start with a joke."

"I need to share all this information."

"The audience has to love me."

But although these are nice-to-have qualities, they play a minuscule role in your ultimate success or failure. Effective communication hinges on one job and one job only:

*Moving your point from your head to your audience's heads.*

That's the ball game. If you deliver your point, you succeed. If you don't deliver your point, you fail—even if you're otherwise hilarious, friendly, attractive, relatable, admirable, knowledgeable, and likable.

If it helps, think of yourself as a bicycle messenger. Your only job is moving your package—your point—from Point A to Point B, from your head to your audience's heads. The only measure of success is whether or not the delivery is successful.

Because this act of delivery is so critical, the only way to know if you meet that goal is to ask someone in your audience, "Did you get my point?" For an even better test, see if that person can accurately express your point back to you.

Other "traditional" measures of success—like compliments, applause, laughter, and smiles—are fairly useless as indicators because they don't tell you if you've successfully delivered your point; they only reflect how much you engaged your audience. That's probably useful feedback for a game show host, but not for someone trying to make a point.

Knowing you have a single, specific job can relieve a lot of anxiety, especially if you're worried about things like your appearance, how nervous you seem, or even a foreign accent you may have. Successful point-making is not about your physical presence; it's about the successful transference of your point. Like the bike messenger, simply deliver the goods and avoid any obstacles in your way.

## Start Strong

The first 15 seconds of making your point are critical. In that quarter-minute, your audience will decide if you're going to be interesting or boring. What you do during that short time can make or break that impression.

Friends and colleagues may be rooting for you. Competitors and detractors might be looking for holes in your argument. But they both have the same wish: "Don't put me to sleep." In more actionable terms: "Make a relevant point."

Starting strong—and keeping people awake—relies on getting to that point quickly. Yet do you know the most common first word of most presentations?

*Hello?* No.

*The?* Nope.

*SO.*

Yes. *So.*

Why do we begin so often with "so"? Probably because it makes us feel like we're continuing a dialogue, which is comfortable, instead of starting a speech, which can be scary.

Here are a few examples of not getting to the point quickly, each leading with a big, fat "So. . . ." Do they sound familiar?

*"So . . . how is everyone?"*

*"So . . . you may be wondering. . . ."*

*"So . . . we were talking yesterday about. . . ."*

*"So . . . let's talk a little about. . . ."*

You can avoid this fate simply by knowing what your first word is—and committing to it being your first word.

For me, often it's "my":

*"My name is Joel Schwartzberg. . . ."*

Or "good":

*"Good morning. My name is Joel Schwartzberg. . . ."*

Or "today":

*"Today I want us to focus on a critical issue in our supply chain...."*

Whatever your first word is, don't say anything until you say that word, and then ideally continue with an opening that establishes three things:

1. Who you are (if you are new to your audience)

2. Your point

3. Why your point is relevant (if it's not already embedded in the phrasing of your point)

Because these opening 15 seconds are so critical, I often recommend memorizing them (which is the first and last time I'll recommend you memorize anything, by the way).

If you like, you can still begin your communication with a humanizing icebreaker—a joke, a funny moment from your morning, or a related news item—but they need to be planned, not winged. Also, recognize that these icebreaking devices are not supporting your points; they're delaying them. So it's best to get in and out of a starting thought efficiently so you can quickly move on to your point.

I believe that the dance came from the people, and that it should always be delivered back to the people.

—Alvin Ailey

# 4

# Sell Your Point

When I worked in the editorial department of a magazine for kids, the company's president decided to have a slick sales trainer teach the basics of closing a deal to our entire staff. He wasn't Alec Baldwin in *Glengarry Glen Ross,* but he was close.

Those of us in editorial thought this was an incredible waste of our time—after all, we thought, sales was the focus of our marketing and advertising staff, not the concern of writers and editors.

But, now looking back, I see the president was right. We were all in the business of selling—some of us were selling ad space; others were selling something even more valuable: ideas.

Good ideas, in the form of points, deserve to be sold, not just shared. So how can you make sure you're truly selling your points instead of sharing them? Read on.

## Avoid the Book Report

Too many speakers don't deliver speeches; they deliver book reports. Book reports simply describe who, what, where, and sometimes how and why. These are rarely actual points, yet often treated as if they were. They also don't necessarily convey the speaker's stake in the subject, the subject's relevance to the audience, or the subject's potential impact.

The difference between delivering a book report and conveying a point is similar to the difference between recounting a movie's plot and convincing someone to see it with you. Or between a nonfiction book's table of contents and its blurb on the inside cover. In both cases, the first is a share, the second a sell.

These book reports can take many forms in a workplace, from status reports to Town Hall presentations to sales pitches. In each one, information is explained, but nothing is proposed. There's no "I believe," only an information dump.

I can usually tell a "sharer" from a seller right off the bat. A sharer will often say:

*Today, I want to talk a little about X.*

Is this person selling anything? Seems not, by that introduction. It seems all he wants to do is throw out a few words and mix them with others' words in the hope some of them stick together and magically produce an action step. After all, he only wants to "talk about it."

Compare that to the seller:

*Today, I'm going to explain why doing X will lead to Y.*

Here are two in-depth examples from my workshops:

**Example One:**

A former client of mine was in the business of selling branded merchandise, including hats, brochures, signs, and pins, all featuring a client's logo. I asked her to give me her best sales pitch. She laid out all of her products and began to describe each one:

*See this hat? This hat will never collapse, is fully adjustable, and can feature your logo permanently stitched to the front. See this pin? It can feature a three-color logo and has a magnetic backing so it won't ruin a shirt or jacket. This banner is made from special material that will resist liquids and wrinkles, and your logo can be printed all over it. . . .*

She went on like that until she had no more items to describe, then stopped.

I told her she did a great job describing these products (think: book report), but there was one thing I never heard her say:

*If you use my services, more people will be exposed to your brand, bringing more people to your product and earning you more money.*

**Example Two:**

Another client of mine worked for a major nonprofit organization dedicated to assisting impoverished women in developing nations across the world. Her job was to convince her bosses to green-light a book idea. This is how she pitched it:

*This book represents our mission perfectly—it tells detailed stories of these brave women, combining rich prose and their own words. Each story features pictures taken by award-winning photographers, and there's a topic index in the back you can use to find issues you care about. It will look beautiful in anyone's home and make a meaningful holiday gift.*

Another book report. She described every relevant detail about the book, but she didn't sell the point. Given the mission of her nonprofit, a stronger sell might have sounded like this:

*This book will expose our mission to key audiences and donors, helping us raise funds that will assist more families in peril.*

Making the leap from sharing to selling doesn't require another college degree, just sharp awareness of your strongest point and its highest value proposition.

In a recent public speaking workshop, I wrote the word SELL in big letters on a large piece of paper and held it up when I felt my students weren't *selling* their ideas. The students made profound changes in tone, body language, volume, and word choice, and the audience immediately felt the impact. These students came in as describers; they left as salespeople.

## Use Selling Language

To ensure my clients do more selling than sharing, I encourage them to adopt these point-forcing power phrases:

I propose . . .

I recommend . . .

I suggest . . .

The brilliance of these simple phrases is that—similar to "I believe"—they force the creation of a true point, and typically a value proposition as well. As a result, people who use these power phrases are often seen as leaders . . . and eventually become them.

Try to insert these phrases when you communicate in any format with both employees and supervisors. You'll find your meetings ending with not just action steps, but true momentum.

I believe that television is the only medium that can truly reach society's lowest common denominator.

—Garry Marshall

# 5

# Tailor
# Your Point

**J**ust like you wouldn't make a sandwich for someone
without knowing what he or she likes, consider the same
precautions with your point's impact on your audience.
Some trainers and consultants boil this down to "Know
your audience," but it's more specific than just knowing
who they are and what they know. It's about knowing what
your audience *wants from you.*

These audience wants vary based on specific settings and situations, and may include the following:

- ▶ Information

- ▶ Insight

- ▶ News or updates

- ▶ Inspiration

- ▶ Appreciation

- ▶ Empathy

- ▶ Explanation

- ▶ Comfort

Ideally, the tone of your communication connects with, or at least addresses, your audience's specific expectation. In other words, don't be the strategist when you need to be the inspirer. Don't be the finger-pointer when you need to be the appreciator. Don't be the challenger when you need to be the encourager.

How do you know you're being the "right" you? Before every event, ask yourself this: "What does this particular audience want and need from me?"

Once you determine what your audience expects from you, make sure it's addressed as part of your overall communication, if not within your point itself. Otherwise, you run the risk of seeming out of touch, no matter how strong your point is.

I believe that, as long as there is plenty, poverty is evil.

—Robert Kennedy

# 6
# Stay
# on Point

One of the great benefits of having a point is that you can always call on it to perform a course-correction if you ramble, lose focus, or otherwise leave the planet of your point like an off-course rocket ship.

First, understand that there's no limit to how many times you can bring up your point or use it to get back on track. Your point can't be overstated because no one ever says this after a presentation: "Great speech, but the speaker made his point too many times." That's like complaining about getting too much good advice.

If you suddenly find yourself lost in space, you can immediately get back to your point using transitions like these:

"My point is this. . . ."

"Here's the thing. . . ."

"Here's the idea to remember. . . ."

Just hit the brakes and get back to your point. Politicians do this all the time as part of their jobs. Make it your job as well.

## Their Point vs. Your Point

Occasionally, you may find yourself in settings where you feel pressure to leave your point to address someone else's. It happens most frequently to conference panelists and TV show guests, but it also happens when you find yourself alone with the opinionated dinner guest everyone else is ignoring.

It's tempting to take his bait—especially if you have an ironclad defense. But realize that the more time you spend defending yourself against his points, the less time you spend conveying your own, which, as you now know, is your single most important job.

Also know that, in most conference and interview settings, panelists and interviewees are not—and should not be—expected to act as talking encyclopedias. If a TV host or conference organizer invites you to participate, she owes you a fair forum to convey your points in connection to the predetermined topic. If you sense other expectations or hidden agendas, I recommend passing on the event.

For some of my clients, interviews can be very adversarial, even hostile. They're often personally attacked for beliefs or affiliations peripheral to their points. When this happens, it's critical that they resist the bait to defend themselves personally and stick to their own points as if those points were life preservers. If someone attacks you personally, it means he won't or can't argue *your* point fairly, which is all the more reason to keep pressing it.

In the political world, this tactic of steering the discussion back to your point is often called a *pivot,* but whereas politicians often pivot to vacuous policy positions or slogans, what you're pivoting to is a substantive proposition based on your experience and expertise. That's nothing to apologize for—it's what you came to do.

If someone is determined to move you off your point to debate his own, consider one of these transitional lines (sometimes called *bridges*) to stand your ground and stay on point:

▶ "I hear what you're saying, but my point is. . . ."

▶ "I know that's a popular perception, but the truth is. . . ."

▶ "This is indeed a gray area, but I believe that. . . ."

▶ "Yes, that may be true. But here's my point. . . ."

▶ "That's untrue. Here's what is true. . . ."

▶ "I'll leave that question to others more qualified to speak on that subject, but what I believe is that. . . ."

If someone attacks you personally, you can even say something like this:

"I understand that something about me offends you deeply—and that's unfortunate—but here's the larger point. . . ."

Whether you're answering a question thrown at you or merely acknowledging it, the key next step is to immediately convey your point with strength. In other words, do the job you came to do.

I believe that good things come to those who work.

—Wilt Chamberlain

# 7

# Strengthen Your Point

**Y**ou've now identified your point, learned how to convey it and stick to it, and realized the imperative of selling it versus sharing it. That knowledge alone puts you way ahead of your competitors and colleagues.

Now it's time for extra credit: *strengthening* your point through key presentational understandings and techniques.

## Power Periods

Many people—people you know, people you report to, even people you admire—end their declarations as if they're questions, using a higher pitch at the end, even though no question was posed. It's often called *uptalk or upspeak.*

Listen for it by saying these two sentences aloud, with particular attention to the punctuation:

"Our customer base has tripled in size?"

"Our customer base has tripled in size."

Some people have an innate ability to end their talks with periods; others can't help but uptalk everything out of their mouths. It's not even connected to experience or other communication skill sets. Some of the most accomplished public speakers are chronic uptalkers, and some of the least experienced speakers I know can easily end their sentences with periods. Whether or not you're a natural uptalker, the habit can be very destructive to the successful conveyance of your point. When you ask a question—even if it only sounds like a question—you're indicating "I'm not sure." But when you end with a period, you're saying, "This I know."

To test this, I have my students listen to me count from one to five two different ways. Afterward, I ask them to tell me which presentation of numbers conveyed the most strength, confidence, and authority.

I say the first line like this:

**1?**

**2?**

**3?**

**4?**

**5?**

I say the second line like this:

**1.**

**2.**

**3.**

**4.**

**5.**

Of the thousands of students who've taken this admittedly unscientific test, an overwhelming majority have felt the second group—the ones ending in periods—sounded stronger, more confident, and more authoritative merely on the basis of ending on a period versus a question mark. Nothing else changed, and keep in mind these weren't even words or ideas—just numbers. The mere *sound* of a question dramatically reduced the strength of the conveyance. This is why correcting uptalk is important.

The first step in shifting from uptalk to what I call "power periods" is training your ear to recognize the question mark. Listen to bosses and colleagues. Listen to news anchors and television hosts. If you can stand it, listen to politicians. Train your ear to listen for uptalk in others, then in yourself.

When you reach the point where you can catch yourself engaging in uptalk, you're at the point where you can train yourself to use a power period instead, especially if your pace is slow enough to take that deliberate step.

The goal isn't to have all of your sentences end with power periods. But can you guess what part of your presentation benefits most from a power period (hint: the most important part of your presentation)?

That's right. Your point.

Three of the best power period users I've ever seen were Presidents Ronald Reagan, Bill Clinton, and Barack Obama. Imagine each of them saying these lines in office:

*"This economic package will dramatically improve the lives of middle-class Americans."*

*"These laws will strengthen our homeland security."*

*"The state of our union is strong."*

I don't think it's a coincidence that these former presidents were—and for Clinton and Obama, still are—among our most admired public speakers. It's not because they were presidents; it's because they each knew how to convey "this I believe."

## There's Something Between Us

Intimate conversations are always more compelling than distant ones. This means speakers should get as close to their audiences as they can (without falling into their laps). President Clinton used this tactic during town hall debates when he physically approached the individuals he was engaging.

The big idea is not just moving closer to your audience, but removing obstacles between yourself and them. Those obstacles include podiums, tables, clipboards, iPads, pens, pointers, clickers, and even your hands.

Truth be told, the reason most speakers hold things in their hands or clasp their hands together is so they can transfer nervous energy onto those objects. Indeed, holding an object can feel very comforting. But the detriments outweigh the benefits when you realize these props are distracting your audience from your point.

This is why TED speakers reject podiums and tables and generally keep their hands separated. It's also why you should move closer to your audience if and when you can, and always speak in the light (even when sharing a projected presentation). Yes, darkness is an obstacle too—how can you champion your point if the audience can't even see you?

Speaking of not being seen, people who call in to business meetings suffer the greatest handicap in successfully making their points. This handicap is somewhat reduced in video meetings, but video callers typically look at their screens, not into their cameras, and thus rarely connect directly to their audiences. If you care about making your point to an individual or a group, it's important to be present, both psychologically and physically.

When I stand to speak, I remove everything from my hands and my pockets, move podiums and tables aside, and even take off my glasses. Basically, I do everything I can to avoid distractions, reduce indications of nervous energy, and create more direct connections between me and my audience.

I know these measures will strengthen my point, or at least reduce the number of obstacles in front of it.

## Turn Up the Volume

The simple act of increasing volume reaps tremendous benefits for anyone trying to convey a point. Yet when I ask my students to deliberately "speak *too* loudly"—without shouting—they rarely do. Most simply can't bring themselves to speak too loudly, even when I beg them. At best, they're a little louder than they normally are, and only for the first few words.

The rare few who can speak inappropriately loudly on command are never able to keep it up. By the sixth word, they're generally either at a perfect volume or still too soft.

So let's first dismiss the notion that you will ever speak too loudly. Most people either can't do it or won't allow themselves to do it because of the self-conscious alarm bells it will set off.

Now consider all of the public speaking errors corrected merely by increasing volume:

► Mumbling

► Speaking too quickly

► Ending sentences with question marks instead of periods

► Talking too quietly

Volume is truly a public speaking gift that keeps giving. When my students simply raise their volume, that change alone makes a profound difference in their projections of strength, competence, and authority.

Speaking loudly not only boosts your points, it can also boost your career. It makes interns sound like managers, and managers sound like vice presidents. And counseling an unassertive employee to be louder is a much more actionable request than asking him to "demonstrate more leadership."

If you're on a microphone or on a teleconference, maintain a loud, strong voice. Too many speakers in these situations drop their voices to a conversational volume, not realizing they're reducing the power of their points as well.

Finally, remind yourself and your staff that the burden of making sure everyone can hear the speaker is entirely on the speaker, not on the audience. This is true even in large rooms and for speakers phoning in. No speaker is entitled to extra accommodation because he happens to be "a quiet person."

## Gender-Specific Challenges

The benefits of volume should apply to both genders equally, but occasionally a female student shares a fear that if she increases her volume, she'll be perceived as "aggressive" or "shrill," which she believes might turn an audience against her.

I don't pretend to be a scholar on the subject of gender bias, but when this happens, I'll often ask her and other female students to share their points at a decibel they consider "inappropriately and uncomfortably loud." Then I survey the room: "Does she sound aggressive?" I ask.

The typical response: a unanimous "no." Are her classmates being politically correct? Perhaps, so I ask another question:

"How *did* she sound?"

Answers that come back usually include these descriptors: "strong," "confident," and "assertive"—all indicators of a well-conveyed point.

This doesn't mean there isn't gender bias out there or that you'll never run into it; there is, and you will. But I believe these biased judgments happen most often when communicators are on the defensive, or on the attack—not when they're busy making their most substantive points. Conversely, the more focused you are on your affirmative point, the less likely you'll be accused of seeming aggressive. And consider recent passionate speeches by women who were universally judged as nothing short of powerful:

▶ Michelle Obama's speech at the 2016 Democratic National Convention. If I've ever seen a perfect speech—from the first word to last—that's the one.

▶ Meryl Streep's acceptance speech for the Cecil B. DeMille Award at the 2017 Golden Globe Awards. If that award sounds familiar, it was the same honor bestowed in 2016 on Denzel Washington, whose acceptance "speech" we looked at in Chapter 2.

▶ Viola Davis's moving acceptance speech while receiving the 2017 Academy Award for Best Actress in a Supporting Role.

If you fear being considered shrill or aggressive, and are considering going softer or "more casual" to avoid it, Google and watch these speeches for inspiration.

My overall suggestion to those who fear such perceptions is to ignore them. Don't customize your conveyance to match unfair biases in your audience—that's their problem, not yours. Your job is to step up, even when your audience's job is to grow up.

## You Want Vocal Fry with That?

Another peril of low volume is falling into a pattern of "croaking." This is often called *vocal fry,* and many people do it subconsciously. Some even do it consciously. If you're unfamiliar with the sound of vocal fry, Google "Faith Salie Vocal Fry" and watch Faith's 2013 YouTube video, featuring textbook vocal fry by the Kardashian sisters. Another famous vocal fryer: Bill Clinton.

It's unclear why some people order up more vocal fry than others, but one of the biggest causes is power failure—lackluster energy directed to your voice. So one antidote is energy in the form of volume. Applying energy and strong articulation are probably the two most effective ways to overcome power failure and vocal fry. In fact, I often tell my clients this before their big speeches: "If you're not tired at the end of this speech, you haven't given it enough power." That doesn't mean you should shout your speeches; it means you should simply put enough strength and air behind your points to give them the power they deserve.

This energy can come from sheer will or a deliberate sugar rush, but it's also boosted by a good night's sleep and a good meal—a lesson you should have learned the hard way in college. Nothing puts an audience to sleep faster than a low-energy speech—regardless of point or subject matter—and vocal fry is a strong indicator of that.

## Pausing for Perfection

It's tempting to believe that, if you pause, the audience will think you've forgotten what you were going to say, like an actor who's forgotten his lines. The pause also feels awkward—your mind is thinking: "Shouldn't I be speaking right now? Shouldn't *someone* be speaking?"

But in reality, pauses are not your enemy; they are your ally.

First, recognize that it takes twice as long for your audience to process a thought as it takes for you to say it. Pauses create important gaps during which that critical understanding can sink in. Consider your points like water being poured into the soil of a potted plant—it takes time for the water to be absorbed and go deep.

When you pause, you also create useful dramatic suspense for your audience—"What will happen next?" The audience will then stay tuned in until your very next word. This is one reason good speakers often pause just before conveying their points.

Handled confidently, pausing also tells your audience, "I'm thinking right now, in front of you," which is very exciting for them. Audiences like "live" experiences, including plays or sporting events, and pausing gives your presentation a spontaneous—versus canned—feel.

Pauses are also the proper substitute for nonsense crutch words like "umm," "ahh," and "uhh." It's hard to simply stop saying those words, but pauses give us an alternative. With practice, you can effect a successful transplant.

But the best reason by far to pause is that it buys you the time you need to construct precise statements. For many of us, our mouths run ahead of our brains, meaning you're saying things before you've fully conceived them. Pausing reverses the order, so that your mind is in front of your mouth, enabling you to fully conceive that idea before conveying it.

Here's a way to test this. Right now, out loud, describe one of the things you most appreciate about your job and why that aspect fulfills you. Begin it like this: "One of the things I most like about being an X is. . . ." (If you hate your job, imagine a better one—this is just an exercise, not a performance review.)

Go ahead. I'll wait.

Done?

Now do it again. But this time, keep this in mind:

*I have all the time in the world and can pause as many times as I need to, and for as long as I need to, to say exactly what I mean.*

Embrace that concept of no-penalty pausing, and try again.

Was there a difference? The pauses should have helped by giving you time to prepare your phrases. If your pauses were very long, practice will help bring them down to a manageable size. And if you're worried about the impact of those pauses, know that an audience rarely says, "That was a great presentation . . . except for all the pausing."

Pauses are rarely remembered by the audience, because, simply, it's hard to remember a moment of nothing. So use pauses to build suspense, to leverage spontaneity, and to create points with precision. It will take some practice, but when you ultimately embrace the pause, it can be one of your point's best friends.

Despite everything, I believe that people are really good at heart.

—Anne Frank

# 8

# Complete Your Point

**W**hen you finish delivering a presentation, the best thing you can end with is your point. It doesn't need to be your very last line (though there's nothing wrong with that), but it should be conveyed in your final moments, because it's what you most want your audience to be thinking about as they leave.

I call this "sticking the landing" because ending on a strong restatement of your point is like an aerial gymnast hitting the mat cleanly, with no extra steps.

When my students don't stick the landing, they're often making one of the following four mistakes:

1. Ending with some variation of "and that's all I got," including my personal favorite "well, that's the last slide" (as if the presentation was a grueling endurance test)

2. Ending without conveying or reiterating a final point

3. Mumbling the last line

4. Never ending decisively at all

The last one merits extra emphasis. Why do some people just go on and on and on, as if cursed to do so? Imagine a pizza delivery person ringing your doorbell. You let him in, get your money, and pay him, including his tip. He hands you the delicious pizza . . . then just stands there, not leaving, not moving at all.

The delivery guy represents a communicator who has just delivered his point . . . and for some reason is *still talking*. The more he talks, the more diluted and distant his point becomes.

To avoid this, be aware of the moment you've successfully conveyed your point. When you get there, stop or conclude quickly to avoid self-sabotage. Deliver the goods, recognize that you have, and get the heck out.

One mistake meeting speakers often make is connecting their final word immediately to another agenda item, such as a Q&A session or the introduction of another speaker.

They allow no time for that final point to sink in. It sounds like this:

> "This approach will help us save more lives than ever before—now let's bring up Sally for our next presentation."

Don't rob emphasis from your point and dilute the impact of your power period by rushing into a housekeeping item. Put a virtual paragraph break between the two:

> "This approach will help us save more lives than ever before."
>
> (beat, probably applause)
>
> " . . . Now I call on Sally to show you how this approach will also save us money."
>
> or
>
> " . . . Now I'm happy to take some questions."

The biggest reason people muff their endings is that they have no clear point to begin with. Without a true point, you have no case to make and thus nothing to offer your audience as you conclude. So the speaker stops abruptly, or goes on and on, in fruitless search of that one idea she meant to convey.

You often see this during wedding toasts, when the speaker thinks his point is simply "Jack, my best friend." Twenty minutes later, it's a rambling mess in search of a real point, and not just because Jack's BFF was drunk.

I believe that a creative career is only as good as the risks you take with it.

—Cate Blanchett

# 9

# Five Enemies of Your Point

Even if you master all of these simple, smart, and practical tips, you may still run into some obstacles when you try to deliver your point. We already talked about what to do if someone tries to drag you off your point, but here are some other less-obvious challenges, many of which come directly from you.

## Enemy #1: "And"

We've all heard that "less is more"—meaning that concise communications have greater impact. But we should also take to heart the idea that "more is less"—meaning that when we add words, we're actually subtracting power from our points.

This might seem counterintuitive. After all, aren't points like houses—increasing in value when we add extensions? Following that idea, many communicators deploy the seemingly innocent word "and" to attach multiple ideas to single points.

The problem is, with each additional "and," you're diluting the power of your point by giving the audience other options to consider.

Look at how I started this chapter's introduction:

> *Even if you master all of these simple, smart, and practical tips ...*

Did you retain the meaning behind all of those adjectives equally? Did you retain the meaning behind any of them for long?

What if I had written the following line instead?

> *Even if you master all of these practical tips ...*

Here I've given your mind a single idea to process, and chances are it'll stick better.

Now see how the "and" affects a more substantial point. Compare the following two lines:

► *This approach will elevate and enhance our ability to be successful and save lives.*

► *This approach will elevate our ability to save lives.*

To my eyes and ears, the second example is much more instantly engaging . . . and this point never needed "enhance" and "successful" in the first place.

In Chapter 2, I called this problem *split ends*, but here I want to focus on how to spot them. It all comes down to the word *and*. Give all of your prepared speeches and reports the "And" Test by asking yourself these two questions each time: Do I need all of these qualifiers? What do I gain and lose by using only the strongest one? Chances are, by dropping extra "ands," you'll gain more than you lose.

This doesn't mean you have to remove all of your "ands," but this test will also help kick out weaker adjectives (bad-jectives), making your point more striking ~~and memorable~~ as a result.

## Enemy #2: Nonsense Words

In Chapter 7, I referred to nonsense words, and it's worth underscoring them here as a clear enemy of your point. Obviously, you want to be making sense, not nonsense. And these words typically fall into the category of nonsense:

- ► Umm
- ► Ah
- ► So

In Toastmasters International, a well-known nonprofit public speaking educational organization, a member assigned the role of "Ah Counter" is charged with the responsibility of literally counting the number of times a speaker utters one of these crutch words.

Although it's important to know how often you use non-sensical crutches—and especially to know what your crutch words are—knowing doesn't always put you on the path to correcting. It's hard to stop doing something, even when you know it's wrong. (I'm thinking of chocolate cake right now. You?)

What you need is something to replace that destructive activity. In this case, the appropriate replacement is the pause. Your goal is to train yourself to sense when a non-sense word is coming and employ a pause instead.

As I mentioned in Chapter 7, a pause is one of your best allies because it creates time for you to plan what to say, ensuring that your next words make sense, not nonsense.

## Enemy #3: All Apologies

One of the few "nevers" I share in workshops is never apologize or even say "excuse me." The problem with public apologies is that they're like a big neon sign around your neck that says, "I messed up." Audiences remember apologies, and the words alone can do serious damage to the credibility you've built up to that point.

Remember that by sharing your valuable points you're doing your audience a favor; your audience is not doing you a favor. So even if you have a word bobble, a cough, a skipped page, or a hiccup, there's no need to apologize or be excused. Just move on. If necessary, make a correction without an apology:

*We had a 35 percent success rate—actually, a 75 percent success rate.*

In a related "never," never say how nervous, unprepared, or intimidated you might be. You may be feeling these things, but don't reveal them, because blurted admissions like these also decimate your credibility.

Consider "I'm nervous" to be code for "I'm not a professional." If you're nervous, just keep plowing through, knowing that it's the delivery of your point that matters, not the impression you're making personally.

## Enemy #4: Speed

Speed kills . . . points. What many speakers don't realize is it takes much longer for an audience to hear and process a point than it takes for them to say it. As a result—especially for fast-talkers like me—audiences have trouble retaining information merely because they don't have enough time to digest it. Fast talkers' mouths are typically running ahead of their minds. This robs the speaker of valuable point-construction time. Ideally, the situation is reversed—your mind is way ahead of your mouth, setting up words and ideas like a volleyball to be spiked moments later.

If you're a fast talker, it won't help for me to simply say, "Follow the speed limit." Speed is hard to control, but brakes are not. In this case, your brakes are volume and pausing. Raising your volume requires more breath, making it difficult to speak quickly. And inserting pauses will break up your pace, giving you critical milliseconds to self-correct and plan your points.

Something I often tell my public speaking students is to consider all audiences *hard-of-hearing* and *very, very dumb*. This presumption forces a speaker to speak slowly, with greater volume, and with simpler language, which is always a good idea, regardless of your audience's IQ.

## Enemy #5: The Department of Homeland Insecurity

Take the number of people you know, subtract the number of in-laws you really like, and multiply it by a schma-billion. Now you have merely a fraction of the number of people frightened by the thought of giving a public presentation.

In many polls, people fear public speaking more than death. But let's be clear—it's not public speaking people fear; it's public humiliation. So the solution isn't avoiding public speaking at all costs; it's avoiding the thought that you can make a complete fool of yourself.

Who tells you when you're making a fool of yourself more often than any other person?

You.

It's the voice inside your head that says

- ▶ "You're screwing up. . . ."
- ▶ "Everyone thinks you're boring. . . ."
- ▶ "You sound silly. . . ."
- ▶ "You look very, very nervous . . . and you should be!"

Because this voice comes from inside and sounds like you, you're inclined to believe what it says. But that voice doesn't come from your head; it comes from your internal Department of Homeland Insecurity (DHI)—where your insecurity lives.

And the person behind the voice? It's the DHI's spokesperson and chief lobbyist. Let's call him Roy. One thing you should know about Roy: He's a liar. He's not just clumsy or mistaken; he's a malicious liar. It's Roy's job to make you feel insecure, to make you second-guess yourself, and to sabotage every effort you make to convey confidence.

So why would you trust him?

I see Roy's influence every time a client stops mid-sentence and sits down, or starts by saying, "This is not going to be very good . . . ," or "Okay, here goes nothing . . . ," or ends with "Well, that sucked" and a scrunched face. Roy is a master at inducing self-sabotage, and he'll lie to create that outcome.

Those butterflies you feel before giving a speech? They aren't in your stomach; they're in your head. And they didn't just hatch there; they were planted. By Roy.

When people ask me how to overcome public speaking anxiety, I focus on three ideas, none of which involve murdering Roy.

1. Know your point. Anyone who doesn't know his or her point *should* be nervous.

2. Know that the moment is not about you, or even your speech; it's about your point. All you have to do is deliver it.

3. Practice out loud—not in your head or by mumbling. The key training is having your mouth and your brain collaborate on the conception and conveyance of a point. That can only happen if you're actually using your mouth.

As I said earlier, the only way to know if you've successfully delivered your point is to approach someone in your audience afterward and ask, "Did you receive and understand my point?" That's it.

All other sources—from Roy, the liar in your head, to the face in your mirror, to the supportive colleague who simply says "you did great!"—are useless in providing accurate assessments of your public speaking success.

I believe the children are our future.
Teach them well and let them lead the way.

—written by Michael Masser and Linda Creed
and sung by Whitney Houston

# 10

# Train Others to Make Points

No matter where they sit in a company hierarchy, *everyone* can benefit from conveying real points. So don't keep these ideas to yourself. Train your staff to identify and strongly convey their own points. Others will notice.

Here are some good ways to start:

- ► When you meet with employees, encourage them to use the point-forcing power phrases like "I recommend" and "I suggest." If they don't do it naturally, make a habit of asking them, "What do you recommend? What do you suggest?" Eventually, they'll get the hint.

▶ Run group exercises in which your staff practices expressing points as "I believe" statements. This is helpful to a group because, in my experience, people learn as much from hearing others formulate points as they do from formulating their own.

▶ Challenge employees to be louder, to embrace pauses, and to find and articulate their highest-value propositions.

▶ Suggest that qualified members of your staff take speaking roles at internal meetings and conferences. Real-world practice builds confidence and strength.

▶ Recommend that those terrified of public speaking join a local Toastmasters International club. What Toastmasters does best is make nervous speakers feel more comfortable about presenting.

▶ Give them this book. It can't hurt.

I believe purpose is something for which one is responsible; it's not just divinely assigned.

—Michael J. Fox

# 11

# Cases in Point

In previous chapters, I covered how to understand, make, and sell your points with the highest impact. Now let's put all these how-to instructions together by applying them to specific scenarios that represent both unique challenges and valuable opportunities.

## Scenario I: Speeches

There's a universe of advice on giving a good speech, but now you understand that what's more important than knowing how to breathe, gesture, stand, and dress sharply is having a real point, using volume, and leveraging pauses. It's one thing to look like you know what you're talking about; it's another to truly convey your point.

Whether you're sweating bullets or cool as a cucumber, here are a few primary questions to ask yourself.

# ☐ Am I reading from a script?

Many people start the journey of giving a speech by making a terrible mistake: they write a speech, word by word.

The truth is, unless you're giving a keynote address or using a teleprompter, you rarely need to write a speech.

The biggest reason not to write a speech is that you don't want to read a speech. Reading forces you to look down often and lose eye contact, and eye contact is crucial to engaging your audience. It's very hard to read to an audience and come across as heartfelt at the same time. The best speeches make it seem like you're spontaneously sharing a fresh idea, not reading from a script written days or weeks ago.

So why do people still rely on writing out their speeches word for word?

Many think they'll score points for being precise and poetic, but here's the thing: The audience is not reading your speech; they're listening to it. By and large, listeners don't remember your words; they remember your points—that is, if you make points. And if you're given a choice between the audience remembering your beautiful words or resonant point, which would you rather have them retain?

If you're writing a script to mitigate your nervousness, you're focusing on the wrong solution and potentially sabotaging your goal. I've seen many speech-readers lose their places in their scripts and have trouble finding them again.

Few things derail a conveyance more than a speaker trying to find her place in a manuscript.

Lack of connection, diminished impact, injured authenticity, and a high chance for error—those are heavy prices to pay for the benefit of simply nailing some words.

## ☐ Did I unveil my point in the first 30 seconds?

Don't treat your point like a climax or spoiler; bring it out early so your audience knows where you're taking them and why.

## ☐ Did I make smart notes for myself?

Once you have your main point and a few examples or subpoints in mind, write them down on a small note card using as few words as possible and no complete sentences. Know that notes have only one purpose: to remind you of the points you need to make and the details you might otherwise forget, like statistics or names. Nothing else belongs in your notes.

I often say the notes should resemble a band's set list—a quick look should instantly provide the key things you need to remember and their order.

Before I assess my clients' speeches, I scan their notes. If I can make enough sense of those notes to give the speech myself, there's too much information, and I ask the client to boil them down further. What I'm looking for are notes that are so cheat-sheet-like that they make no sense to anyone but the speaker.

As practice progresses, speakers should pay attention to how little they rely on their notes, and rewrite them accordingly. What starts as a full-page outline should eventually become a five-bullet note card.

One very serious mistake people make with notes is looking at their notes while they're talking, as if the notes are the audience. But everything you're directing into that piece of paper is information you're not giving your audience. And I'll tell you right now, your notes couldn't care less.

Remember that audiences don't remember pauses, so when you look down at your notes, don't be afraid to pause until you see what you need to see; then look up and deliver the idea.

## ☐ Can I just wing it?

Some people think their vast knowledge or experience imbues them with the innate ability to communicate that knowledge effectively. I've seen it time and time again—particularly from lawyers and professors—and it's almost always a recipe for a rambling disaster.

One senior executive I knew years ago enjoyed following up big staff presentations with "a thought or two" that typically lasted an hour or more. With his prepared notes rolled up in his hand, he went on to share what he thought was an inspiring stream of insight. At best, he did no harm, but few things he said, if any, were remembered or had any meaningful impact. At worst, his audience resented him making them suffer the rhetorical equivalent of waterboarding.

Bottom line: If what you're about to do feels like you're winging it, stop everything. Identify your biggest point, lead with it, and keep supporting it.

## ☐ Did I practice right?

You know practice is important, but as I mentioned earlier, mumbling your speech to yourself is not useful practice. It's what people do when they try to memorize . . . which is not what you're trying to do.

The critical part of practice is when you actually deliver the speech out loud, with full words and sentences. It doesn't require a camera, a mirror, or a colleague—just speaking in full voice.

Some people practice with video, which is a necessary tool for media training and an optional one for public speaking training. I don't traditionally use video in my workshops for two reasons:

1. When we look at ourselves on video, we never ask, "Am I making my point effectively?" Instead, we assess images of ourselves as we've done with cameras and mirrors over the course of our lifetimes, asking "Is my hair in place? Do I look silly? Are my teeth white?" This inclination toward vanity makes it challenging to use video as a tool for improving the conveyance of points.

2. Video can point out weaknesses, but merely *knowing* your weaknesses—for example, knowing how

many times you say "umm"—doesn't help you self-correct. The advice in this book is designed to help you strengthen yourself from the inside out.

## ☐ Do I tell a strategic story?

Audiences love stories. You'll read that in most contemporary articles about public speaking. But a story without relevance is just a story, nothing more. When you choose to use a story to support a point, you need two things:

1. A "strategic story"—one that proves, clarifies, or illustrates your point, not one that's simply an entertaining diversion.

2. An understanding that your story's purpose is not fulfilled until you've explicitly connected it to your point. Too many times I see an executive tell a story but not explain its relevance. That relevance should sound something like this: "I shared this story because it illustrates how. . . ." Without that contextualization, you're relying on your audience to do the heavy lifting—processing your point—themselves.

Let me illustrate this in hypothetical examples:

► A CEO's story about her first job should illustrate her appreciation of hard work . . . and she needs to say that.

► An insurance salesperson's story of an earthquake should illustrate the need for people to prepare for disasters . . . and he needs to say that.

▶ An animal welfare advocate's story of a rescued pit bull should illustrate the need for stronger animal cruelty laws . . . and she needs to say that.

## Scenario 2: PowerPoint

Some people see PowerPoint as a rigid tool that forces unimaginative structure. Fair enough, but smart structure can significantly boost a point by lining up evidence, illustrations, and subpoints to support it.

Effective PowerPoint presentations also keep the speaker on track and visually reinforce points made, whether in words, photos, or charts. This reinforcement is especially important for visual learners—people who learn best by seeing. I know this because I'm a visual learner. When I see points reinforced onscreen, they sink in more. When I'm forced to only listen, I remember less.

But to have a true impact, PowerPoint presentations must meet some specific standards. The following suggestions aren't all the tips and tricks to using PowerPoint—entire books are devoted to that—but they are critical to conveying your point.

### ☐ Does each slide contribute to my overall point?

Each and every side following your title slide should support your major point. If you can't articulate how a slide supports your point, consider reimagining or cutting it.

And if your Title Slide has your point baked in, you'll hit the ground running in terms of engaging your audience. Compare these two slides:

**Leveraging Social Media**

versus

*Leveraging Social Media to Increase Brand Affinity*

## ☐ Am I prepared to explain the relevance of each slide?

Each PowerPoint slide can put forth information, ideas, points, even suggestions, but only you can drive home relevance. For all its bells and whistles, PowerPoint can't do that.

So after you show each slide, say something like, "This is relevant because it (demonstrates how/proves that/supports my point that) XYZ."

This need for explicit relevance is true even for slides that focus on background or history.

Just compare this spoken introduction

> *Let's start with a little bit of history. In 2012 ...*

to this more point-specific one:

> *Reviewing the history of this project will provide us with a meaningful baseline against which we can measure our success. In 2012 ...*

## ☐ Did I remove or shorten all complete sentences?

Avoid extraneous words in your PowerPoint slides. Remember: With PowerPoint, you're simply visually reinforcing the ideas you're conveying orally, which should never require complete sentences.

## ☐ Do I use bullets to break up my subpoints, and did I follow the five-and-five rule?

The *five-and-five rule* dictates that a PowerPoint slide should have no more than five bulleted lines and no more than five words per line. I agree with that, give or take a word or line.

Not only will bullets keep your conveyances succinct, but they'll also ensure your audience spends more time looking at you and less time reading your slides.

## ☐ Are my words and charts readable from the back of the room?

If an audience member can't read your words and graphics from the back of the room, they're too small. It's better to have two to three readable slides than a single one that's only legible to the front row. No presenter should ever be compelled to say, "I know this chart may be hard to read, but. . . ." #EPICFAIL.

## ☐ Do I have useless slides?

To me, a slide is useless if it doesn't clearly support your point, so I recommend cutting slides that don't meet that standard.

Some presentation gurus recommend slides that contain only a single word like "GRIT" or "INNOVATE," or cryptic-but-cool phrases like "FOLLOW YOUR KITE." They argue that audiences will remember these simple phrases more than they will a list of bulleted content.

Maybe they will, but consider these points:

▶ Even if the audience remembers "GRIT" or "FOL-LOW YOUR KITE," what will those ideas mean once they're separated from their context? What value will they have? Probably as much as the last proverb you pulled from a fortune cookie.

▶ A presentation isn't a memory test. Audiences often take notes and can typically get the PowerPoint decks afterward. So why subject them to relatively pointless pages when you could be sharing pages with substance?

▶ It bears repeating: A communicator's job is to convey points, not throw out words.

## ☐ Are my slides supporting me or am I supporting my slides?

Often I see speakers at the far side of the room or even in their seats, clickers in hand, reading their slides as they click through them. Or I notice speakers presenting in darkness so their PowerPoints can be illuminated.

In each of these scenarios, the speaker has ceded his crucial role as point conveyer—as well as all the authority and credibility attached to that role—to a piece of technology.

The speaker is diminished and the PowerPoint exalted.

If you're one of these people, you should find this transference of ownership offensive. Your PowerPoint deck didn't get a college degree, never really worked a day in its life, and is nowhere near as educated, qualified, and credible as you are. So why are you taking the back seat?

Good presenters don't let their tech toys make points on their behalf. They stand in the center of the speaking area, fully in the light, conveying points supported by the slides behind them.

When I use PowerPoint, I don't even mind blocking the audience's view of the screen. I know they'll see it eventually, and my primary goal is for them to get my points directly from me, the most qualified person to do that job. The technology always plays a supporting role.

## Scenario 3: Making Points in Email

Making points clearly in email is as important as it is in any other form of communication. But too often, emailers make mistakes that seriously detract from the impressions their points leave on readers. Here's a checklist I run through before I hit "send" to make sure I'm conveying my points in the strongest way possible.

### ☐ Is my point in the subject line?

Email subject lines are a prime location for hinting at points within. Aim toward being clear and concise to make the best use of the space ("Thoughts on Infrastructure Proposal"), and don't be afraid to change a thread's subject line if it has become obsolete or if you're taking it in a new direction. Nothing is more misdirecting than a new thought living under an old subject line.

### ☐ Could this be better explained in bullets?

If you're wondering whether or not to use bullets, the answer is probably yes. Bullets are a point's flashlight. They say, "Look here; appreciate this." A good approach is to state your point clearly, then make your case in bulleted items:

*Using our in-house talent is a good idea because it will*

▷ *Eliminate markups from expensive vendors*

▷ *Create new opportunities for staff development and skill diversification*

▷ *Enable us to control the project from beginning to end and make as many revisions as we feel necessary*

As a reader, compare that example to this unbulleted version:

*This in-house approach will benefit the company because it will eliminate the need for expensive vendors who often mark up the cost of their services, create new opportunities for staff development and expand their range of skills, and enable us to control the project from beginning to end as well as make as many revisions as we deem necessary.*

Which approach leaves you with a clearer understanding of the emailer's argument?

## ☐ If I raised an issue, did I suggest a solution?

A former supervisor of mine mandated that anyone making a criticism must also offer a corrective suggestion, or better yet, phrase the criticism as a suggestion. That rule made an enormous difference in both the productivity and morale of our staff meetings. No one likes a hit-and-run naysayer, and constructive points ("I believe we should do this," not "I believe we shouldn't have done that") are more easily received and likely to inspire action.

## ☐ Do I have paragraphs longer than three sentences?

Unless you're sharing gossip, your audience's interest will start to wane somewhere between sentence four and five. So break up long paragraphs to keep their interest. Paragraph breaks are like tiny chapter changes—each one kickstarts the reader's attention.

## ☐ Are my facts correct?

Like (most) news outlets, business emails rely on credibility. And credibility comes from an implicit trust that the sender is sharing truth, not alternative facts. So be your own fact-checker, and make sure you can stand behind your points.

## ☐ Did I check for grammatical errors?

Spelling and grammar mistakes can be huge distractions and even injure your credibility. Always reread and spell check your emails before you send them. If you want to be extra careful, review your email again in a different or larger font for a fresh look at the content.

## ☐ Did I end with a suggestion, a recommendation, or a proposal?

Remember, your point needs to be sold, not just shared. So why leave the next step to chance? Reinforce your point with a specific recommendation or suggestion, whether it's "Let's meet again next Thursday" or "I suggest we have Alyssa put together a project plan."

## Scenario 4: Staff Meetings

Most of the points you make won't be in front of 100 people in an auditorium. More likely, you'll be sitting in a conference room with fewer than 10 people (and a few on the phone pretending to pay attention).

In this setting, most of the rules I've discussed for conveying points still apply, particularly these:

▶ Know your point.

▶ Prepare in advance.

▶ Be loud.

▶ Use pauses for precision.

▶ Say "I recommend" and "I propose."

▶ Mind your word economy.

▶ Remember your #1 job: deliver your point.

It may help to write points into your notebook or laptop ahead of time and bring them to the meeting with you. These notes will support you when you need to make your point, and as long as you're not reading them, they will seem spontaneous. No "winging it" necessary.

## Scenario 5: Executive Internal Communications

Executive managers are responsible for a number of important internal communications, including routine speeches, staff meetings, event remarks, and all-staff memos. The subjects covered can range from Employee Appreciation Day to full-scale reorganizations. But as diverse as these moments are, they each have common obligations—starting with having a defined point in the first place.

Consider this statement:

> *Let's celebrate Employee Appreciation Day!*

versus

> *Let's spend Employee Appreciation Day recognizing outstanding colleagues.*

and

> *This reorganization is good for the company.*

versus

> *This reorganization will allow us to allocate more resources to our life-saving mission.*

The following are some other self-checks that can strengthen critical points coming from the biggest boxes on the org chart.

## ☐ Did I bury my point?

Journalists are criticized for "burying the lead" when they expound too much before revealing their main point. What should be in line one or two ends up all the way down in paragraph two, often because the writer was enamored by his own introductory fluff.

Executives will often do the same thing—bury their points in attempts to "set the stage" or "warm up the audience." In so doing, they risk misleading the audience and diluting their key messages.

Revealing your primary point early works well as part of a preview: "This is what I'm going to show you."

Here's an example:

> *Dear Staff,*
>
> *I love time-saving tools because they allow us to work more efficiently. So I'm excited to share recent improvements to our IT products and cloud-based services, as well as staff shifts in the IT department, that I believe put us on an easier path to doing our best work.*

A quick recommendation: use the present tense. These are active communications, so if you feel inclined to write or say, "I wanted to tell you," consider changing to "I want to tell you." Seems like a minor thing, but you would never say "I was proud to share with you . . . " or "I was excited to announce . . . ," so don't put your "want" in the past. Always put yourself in the moment.

## ☐ Did I keep it tight?

Brevity is a virtue, and most staffers want to go back to their work quickly after reading an announcement or attending a meeting. So show appreciation for their time by getting to the point quickly, saying your thanks, and then getting out of the way (don't be the pizza guy).

Look for words—particularly badjectives—you can cut, and second-guess sections that sound good to you but are more "neat to know" than "need to know."

## ☐ Did I end with aspiration?

A good way to build inspiration is by conveying aspiration—what you hope to ultimately accomplish that will benefit the staff and the company's bottom line. It's also motivating to end on a hopeful note. So dig deep for the most hopeful version of you, and incorporate the hard work of your staff in that point:

> *I believe that our biggest accomplishments are just around the corner. Seeing how committed and excited you are, I know we will get there.*

## ☐ Did I remember to say thanks?

One of the most valuable concepts a boss can convey to employees—and possibly the easiest as well—is appreciation. To her staff, a chief's thanks is a box of chocolates covered in gold stars. Executives should include appreciation in every communication, whether it's posed to staff in general ("I saw great commitment") or points out particular efforts ("I'd like to spotlight Jen's huge impact").

Because executive acknowledgment has such an impact—putting the staff on the executive's side and capturing their attention right off the bat—it's an outstanding way to introduce or boost a key point with a simple transition:

> *The IT team's outstanding commitment demonstrates how beneficial it is to evolve from within.*

# Scenario 6: Performance Reviews

Giving effective verbal performance reviews shouldn't be taken for granted. Reviewing staff performance is not just about staff development and promotion; it's also about executives ensuring they get the support they need to do their own jobs successfully. And successful reviews hinge on the conveyance of clear and concise points.

## ☐ Did I start with a general overview?

There's no need to keep your employees in suspense. Start with a broad but clear point that ties to a goal, like this:

> *Charlie, [I believe] your overall work has been effective and has contributed to our success identifying new markets for our widgets.*

This will immediately break the ice and put your employee at ease.

If your comments are mostly negative, be just as clear about that point and its impact on the goal.

> *Charlie, [I believe] your overall work has fallen just short of our expectations, so let's use this opportunity to discuss ways to improve your approach and productivity toward finding new markets for our widgets.*

## ☐ Did I clearly communicate my employee's challenges and offer examples?

As you share challenges and suggested improvements, make sure to offer examples. This is not the time to re-litigate those moments, however. Your intention is to improve your employee's performance, not to invite debate. If your employee takes a defensive stance, be clear about your goal:

*I hear what you're saying and appreciate your perspective. But right now, my intention is to focus on how we can best move forward.*

## ☐ Did I offer recommendations for improvement?

As I mentioned earlier, one of my favorite supervisors trained his staff to never offer criticism without proposing a solution. This advice is as beneficial for a performance review as it is for a staff meeting. Sometimes the solution will come from your experience, sometimes as a recommendation from your HR or Learning and Development department, and sometimes from brainstorms with your employee.

Recommending avenues for improvements is connected to making points because, as you know by now, just saying "I recommend" forces you to make a strong point.

## Scenario 7: Conference Panels

If you're relatively successful or famous, or you're just LinkedIn friends with an event organizer, sooner or later you'll be asked to sit on a conference panel. Some people think being a panelist is easier than being a speaker, but consider all the obligations: asserting your key points; responding to live questions; appearing both knowledgeable and open to ideas; comfortably interacting with panelists, the moderator, and the audience; and carefully straddling that line between saying too much and too little.

Just as with a speech, success as a panelist is dependent on your ability to identify and convey your key points. If the session ends without you selling those points, you might as well have not been there at all. No matter what else happens during that hour—irrelevant questions from the moderator, combative reactions from the audience, grandstanding by a co-panelist—it's your job to make sure you do what you came to do.

Because of all these moving parts, preparation is critical—and yet often overlooked. "I can wing it," say some panelists, thinking expertise and knowledge alone can carry them. Very often, they crash and burn.

This checklist will help you stay on point while in the chair.

## ☐ Did I prepare my points in advance?

Never go in cold. Prepare two or three points in advance that relate to your expertise and the mission of the conference or event. Consider and explain how these points can tangibly help the audience, and focus on the "need to know" more than the "neat to know."

If you can, mention these points to your moderator in advance, so she can prompt you. Your moderator is just as interested in your ability to make meaty points as you are.

## ☐ Do I know who I answer to?

Unless you've been instructed otherwise, always respond to whoever asks the question. Moderator questions go back to the moderator. Panelist questions go back to the panelist. Audience questions go back to the audience.

You can throw some of that love to your audience—especially if you're offering a value proposition that applies to them—but your opening and closing focus should be on the person asking the questions.

## ☐ Do I know everyone's names?

Memorize the moderator's and your co-panelists' names, and use them frequently. Collegiality—even phony collegiality—projects a level of comfort that exudes confidence. But don't take chances. Calling a panelist by the wrong name has the same effect as calling your romantic partner by the wrong name: once you make that mistake, your credibility is toast, and even your points can't help.

## ☐ Do I have supporting data in my head?

Your credibility as a panelist comes from your qualifications (which should be established in the conference program or by your moderator), your smart points (which is on you), and your supporting data. Don't leave that third part to chance. Keep data, case studies, and specific examples in mind—and in your notes—and be prepared to raise them and connect them explicitly to your point. Few things get an audience's attention more than the words, "What we learned from this case study is. . . ."

## ☐ Am I ready to jump in?

If you don't get your point in early, you may need to fight a little bit on its behalf. Consider the occasion more like a dinner party than a spelling bee—turns aren't important. Use connectors like "Building on Sarah's point . . . " or "I'd like to go back to something Jacob said . . . " or "One point I want your audience to leave with is. . . ."

Remember: If the session ends without you making your point, it's a wasted opportunity, no matter what else came out of your mouth.

## ☐ Did I bring a strategic story?

Just like with a speech, a relevant personal story—the more personal, the better—can go a long way toward illustrating your point and improving its resonance. Just remember that the story only has value when you explicitly explain its relevance to your point.

## ☐ Am I conveying my points or rebutting theirs?

As I mentioned earlier, if the conversation takes a wrong turn, don't follow it down that rabbit hole. Steer it back to your points with a transition like this:

> "That's an important issue, but let's remember the key point: [*point*]."

> "I hear you. But my point of view is that [*point*]."

> "There's been a lot of conversation about this, but here's the thing: [*point*]."

If you're under attack, defend or restate your points, but don't get defensive and waste time arguing their points.

Remember: Being combative—although exciting for an audience—is almost always a losing proposition for your credibility and your ability to successfully convey your points.

## ☐ Am I showing the audience respect?

Panel discussion audiences, like romantic partners, want to be acknowledged. But you can't butter them up with flowers and candy. Below are the gifts they like, whether they know it or not.

Compliments: *"Good question!"*

Restating their question: *"What I hear you asking is. . . ."*

Referring to them later: *"This connects to the question asked earlier. . . ."*

Offering substantive insight: *"Here's something you should know."*

For bonus points, follow up your point with a helpful piece of advice. Conference audiences are always looking for valuable things to take back to their cubicles—and not just branded flash drives—so concentrate on the WIIFM: What's in it for me?

A good WIIFM often begins with "Here's something I recommend you do once you get back to your offices. . . ."

## ☐ Am I speaking in complete sentences?

Answering in complete sentences is a good idea for many reasons. First, it enables your point to be clear even to those who missed hearing the question. It also creates more time for you to fully conceive your response while you're talking, and it helps you frame your idea as a point versus a reaction.

**Example:**

*Q: Bob, do you think social media has enhanced our democracy?*

▶ **Bob's "Meh" Response:**

*Sure it has. Just look at how much was inspired by the past election. In fact, where I work, we designed an awesome social media platform.*

▶ **Bob's Better Response:**

*Yes, I absolutely believe social media has the power to enhance our democracy. Just look at all the social conversations inspired by the past election. In fact, at Green Poodle Digital, we designed a highly interactive forum to encourage the exchange of meaningful ideas.*

## ☐ Am I responding or reacting?

A response is a point formulated to fill a knowledge gap with targeted insight: "Here's what I believe." A reaction is a more spontaneous reply, sometimes emotionally driven and defensive: "No, that's not true at all!"

Try to avoid knee-jerk reactions. The moderator and audience may hope for clash and heat, but your job is to craft thoughtful points. The more calm and controlled you are, the easier that job will be.

## ☐ Am I aware of myself?

Remember, the audience is always watching you (and cameras may be as well), so for as long as you're in that seat, look interested, nod at others' good points, and don't do anything that would embarrass your mother if she were in the audience.

Speaking of your mom, some of her other rules also apply here:

- ► Speak up.

- ► Sit up straight.

- ► Don't talk when others are talking.

- ► Don't touch your face.

I believe that anyone can conquer fear by doing the things he fears to do, provided he keeps doing them.

—Eleanor Roosevelt

# Conclusion

L et's revisit Einstein's quote from the very front of this book:

*If you can't explain it simply, you don't understand it well enough.*

Einstein knew—and you know—that ideas are powerful things. But that power is merely potential until you wield it with strategic precision, which means you need to understand the ideas thoroughly.

Many communicators fall short of their point-making potential by leading with half-baked notions instead of points, and by sharing ideas weakly instead of selling them with strength. But people who champion their ideas sway minds, galvanize people, and make a difference. History proves that point over and over. And if all that doesn't move you, perhaps this reminder will:

*Without a point, everything you say is pointless.*

I believe that anyone can become such a champion, once pointed in the right direction. So good luck getting to your point, and please share these tactics with someone you want to see succeed.

# Recommended Reading

Berkun, Scott. *Confessions of a Public Speaker.* Sebastapol, CA: O'Reilly Media, 2011.

Carver, Raymond. *Where I'm Calling From: Selected Stories.* Franklin Center, PA: The Franklin Library, 1988.

Duarte, Nancy. *Resonate: Present Visual Stories That Transform Audiences.* Hoboken, NJ: John Wiley and Sons, 2010.

Heinrichs, Jay. *Thank You for Arguing.* New York: Three Rivers Press, 2007.

Hugo, Victor. *Les Misérables.* New York: Signet, 1862.

Kipfer, Barbara Ann (Princeton Language Institute), ed. *Roget's 21st Century Thesaurus,* 3rd ed. New York: Dell, 2005.

Reynolds, Garr. *Presentation Zen.* Berkeley, CA: New Riders, 2011.

Safire, William. *Lend Me Your Ears: Great Speeches in History.* New York: W. W. Norton & Company, 2004.

Strunk Jr., William, and E. B. White. *The Elements of Style.* Needham Heights, MA: Allyn & Bacon, a Pearson Education Company, 1979.

# About the Author

**Joel Schwartzberg** is the Senior Director of Strategic and Executive Communications for the American Society for the Prevention of Cruelty to Animals (ASPCA) and has been teaching effective presentation and messaging techniques to corporate, group, and individual clients since 2006.

As a public speaking competitor, Joel won the 1990 U.S. National Championship in After-Dinner Speaking and the 1990 Massachusetts State Championship in Persuasive Speaking, and that same year, he was ranked among the top ten collegiate public speakers in the country.

After coaching public speaking teams at the University of Pennsylvania, Seton Hall University, St. Joseph's University, and the City University of New York, Joel was inducted into the National Forensic Association Hall of Fame in 2002.

A father to three, husband to one, and indentured servant to more rescued cats than he cares to reveal, Joel has been published in outlets such as *The New York Times*

*Magazine, Newsweek,* and *New Jersey Monthly.* He is also the author of two award-winning collections of humorous personal essays. He can be reached through his website at www.joelschwartzberg.net.

# Index

five-and-five rule, 85–86
readability, 86
sentence length, 85
slides, 83–88
using, 83
practicing
out loud, 70
speeches, 81–82
public speaking. *See*
speaking

# R

Reagan, Ronald, 48
Roosevelt, Eleanor, 104

# S

Salie, Faith, 53
scripts, reading from, 78–79
selling language, using, 33. *See also* words
selling points, avoiding book
reports, 30–32
sentences, ending, 50
sharers versus sellers, 30–32
"So," avoiding starting with, 26
"So What" test, 11–13
speaking, practicing out loud, 70
speaking quickly, correcting, 50
speaking quietly, correcting, 50
speeches
making notes, 79–80
practicing, 81–82
reading from scripts, 78–79
telling strategic stories,
82–83
unveiling points, 79
winging it, 80–81
speed, 67–68

split ends, avoiding, 15–16, 65
staff, training to convey points,
73–74
staff meetings, 91
standing while speaking,
49–50
starting strong, 25–27
"sticking the landing," 59–60
stories, telling, 82–83. *See also*
personal stories; strategic
stories
strategic stories, telling,
82–83, 99
Streep, Meryl, 52–53
strength, conveying, 46–47
success, measures of, 25
Swift, Taylor, 19–20

# T

Taylor vs. Denzel, 19–21
TED speakers, 49
tests
"I Believe That," 9–13
"So What," 11–13
"Why," 13–15
themes, 8
thoughts, processing by
audiences, 54
titles, 8
Toastmasters International,
65–66, 74
topics, 8

# U

uptalk and upspeak, 46

# V

value proposition, adding,
16–18

vendors, 8
video, practicing with,
81–82
vocal fry, 53–54
volume
    croaking, 53
    increasing, 50–51

## W

Washington, Denzel, 20–21
"Why" test, 13–15
winging it, 80–81
words, detaching from, 18–21.
    *See also* first word; nonsense
    words; selling language

# Berrett–Koehler
## Publishers

**Berrett-Koehler** is an independent publisher dedicated to an ambitious mission: *Connecting people and ideas to create a world that works for all.*

We believe that the solutions to the world's problems will come from all of us, working at all levels: in our organizations, in our society, and in our own lives. Our BK Business books help people make their organizations more humane, democratic, diverse, and effective (we don't think there's any contradiction there). Our BK Currents books offer pathways to creating a more just, equitable, and sustainable society. Our BK Life books help people create positive change in their lives and align their personal practices with their aspirations for a better world.

All of our books are designed to bring people seeking positive change together around the ideas that empower them to see and shape the world in a new way.

And we strive to practice what we preach. At the core of our approach is Stewardship, a deep sense of responsibility to administer the company for the benefit of all of our stakeholder groups including authors, customers, employees, investors, service providers, and the communities and environment around us. Everything we do is built around this and our other key values of quality, partnership, inclusion, and sustainability.

This is why we are both a B-Corporation and a California Benefit Corporation—a certification and a for-profit legal status that require us to adhere to the highest standards for corporate, social, and environmental performance.

We are grateful to our readers, authors, and other friends of the company who consider themselves to be part of the BK Community. We hope that you, too, will join us in our mission.

### A BK Business Book

We hope you enjoy this BK Business book. BK Business books pioneer new leadership and management practices and socially responsible approaches to business. They are designed to provide you with groundbreaking and practical tools to transform your work and organizations while upholding the triple bottom line of people, planet, and profits. High-five!

# Berrett–Koehler
# Publishers

Connecting people and ideas
to create a world that works for all

Dear Reader,

Thank you for picking up this book and joining our worldwide community of Berrett-Koehler readers. We share ideas that bring positive change into people's lives, organizations, and society.

**To welcome you, we'd like to offer you a free e-book.** You can pick from among twelve of our bestselling books by entering the promotional code **BKP92E** here: http://www.bkconnection.com/welcome.

When you claim your free e-book, we'll also send you a copy of our e-newsletter, the *BK Communiqué*. Although you're free to unsubscribe, there are many benefits to sticking around. In every issue of our newsletter you'll find

- A free e-book
- Tips from famous authors
- Discounts on spotlight titles
- Hilarious insider publishing news
- A chance to win a prize for answering a riddle

Best of all, our readers tell us, "Your newsletter is the only one I actually read." So claim your gift today, and please stay in touch!

Sincerely,

Charlotte Ashlock
Steward of the BK Website

Questions? Comments? Contact me at bkcommunity@bkpub.com.

Certified
Corporation
bcorporation.net